FIRST AMERICANS
The Zuni

TERRY ALLAN HICKS

Marshall Cavendish
Benchmark
New York

ACKNOWLEDGMENTS

Series consultant: Raymond Bial

The craft on pages 20 to 21 was adapted from Marian Broida's *Projects about the Plains Indians* (Marshall Cavendish, 2004).

Marshall Cavendish Benchmark
99 White Plains Road
Tarrytown, New York 10591
www.marshallcavendish.us

Text, maps, and illustrations copyright © 2010 by Marshall Cavendish Corporation
Map illustrations by Rodica Prato
Craft illustrations by Chris Santoro

Library of Congress Cataloging-in-Publication Data
Hicks, Terry Allan.
The Zuni / by Terry Allan Hicks.
p. cm. — (First Americans)
Includes bibliographical references and index.
Summary: "Provides comprehensive information on the background, lifestyle,
beliefs, and present-day lives of the Zuni people"—Provided by publisher.
ISBN 978-0-7614-4137-3
1. Zuni Indians—History—Juvenile literature. 2. Zuni Indians—Social
life and customs—Juvenile literature. I. Title.
E99.Z9H53 2008
978.9004'97994--dc22
2008041998

Front cover: A Zuni boy performs the Rainbow Dance at a tribal event in Gallup, New Mexico
Title page: A Zuni "beehive" oven
Photo research by: Connie Gardner
Cover photo by Chuck Place/Alamy

The photographs in this book are used by permission and through the courtesy of: NativeStock: Marilyn Angel Wynn, 1, 11, 21; Tom Bean Photography: 4, 22, 32, 40; Bridgeman Art Library: William Robinson Leigh/Zuni Pottery Maker, 9; The Granger Collection: 34, 35; Associated Press: Kamenko Pajie, 39; Alamy Images: Lebrecht Music and Arts Photo Library, 25; North Wind Picture Agency, 41; Art Resource: Werner Forman, 10; Jupiter Images: Index Stock Imagery, 28; Getty Images: National Geographic, 12; Transcendental Graphics, 27; North Wind Picture Agency; 14, 16; Corbis: Timothy H. O'Sullivan, 19; Danny Lehman, 24.

Editor: Deborah Grahame
Publisher: Michelle Bisson
Art Director: Anahid Hamparian
Series Designer: Symon Chow

Printed in Malaysia
1 3 5 6 4 2

CONTENTS

1 · WHO ARE THE ZUNI?

The high deserts of the American Southwest have always been a harsh, difficult place for human beings to live. The summers are brutally hot, the winters bitterly cold, and food and water scarce. Yet Native American peoples have lived here for thousands of years. Some of the most successful at surviving in this harsh environment—and holding on to their traditional way of life—are the Zuni (ZOO-nee) or Zuñi (ZOO-nyee) people.

The Zuni belong to a group of Native Americans known as the **Pueblo**, from a Spanish word meaning "village." The Pueblo peoples lead a **sedentary**, or settled, way of life, living in permanent villages. They are closely related to one another by their traditions, such as farming, pottery making, and similar religious practices. But they do not necessarily share common ancestors or speak related languages.

Corn Mountain rises high above the desert at Zuni Pueblo.

Most of the Pueblo live in the present-day state of New Mexico, especially along the Rio Grande. (One group of Pueblo people, the Hopi, lives in Arizona.) The Zuni lands once covered a huge area of the Southwest. Today the Zuni live in a single **pueblo** in the northwestern corner of New Mexico, along the Zuni River, near the town of Gallup. The pueblo lies in a small valley that has rich, fertile soil and is surrounded by flat-topped mountains called mesas.

The Zuni, like all Native Americans, are descendants of ancient peoples who are believed to have walked across a "land bridge" that once connected Siberia and Alaska, beginning sometime between 20,000 BCE and 100,000 BCE. Some of these "**Paleo-Indians**" were living in the southwestern desert as early as 15,000 years ago.

These early peoples were hunters and gatherers who led a **migratory** way of life, moving from place to place in search of food. By about 2000 BCE, however, they had begun to grow corn. They eventually began to build permanent dwellings, called **pit houses**. These were large holes in the ground covered

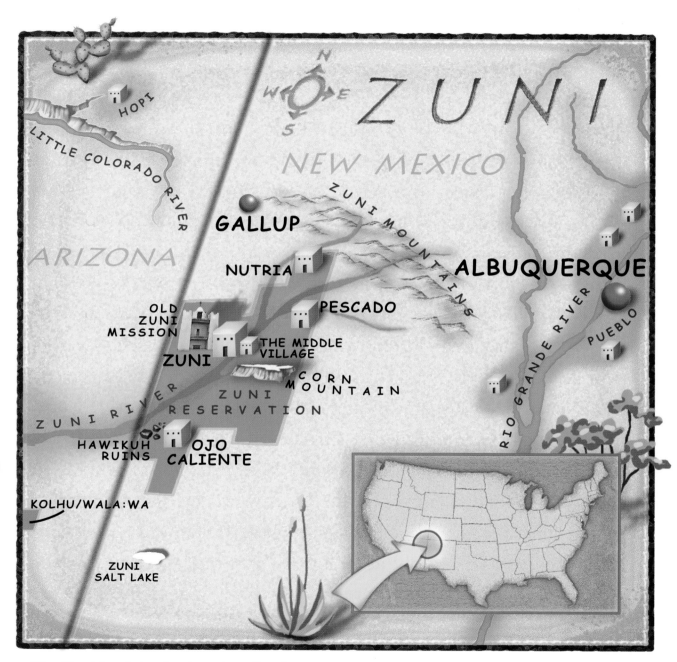

The Zuni lands in the American Southwest

with roofs of wood and **adobe**, a building material made of clay and straw and dried in the sun.

By 700 CE, the Pueblo culture was already highly developed. The Pueblo peoples were living in villages close to their fields of corn, beans, squash, and other **crops**. They were skilled farmers and pottery-makers. Their small villages were also growing larger. They began to build stone houses above ground, although they kept pit house–like structures—known as **kivas**—for religious ceremonies.

One of the great Pueblo mysteries centers on a remarkable people we know as the **Anasazi** or "Ancient Pueblo." Between the 700s and 1300s, the Anasazi built extraordinary multistory dwellings—like modern-day high-rise apartment buildings—into the cliffs at Chaco Canyon in New Mexico. They raised crops and traded them with other Native American peoples living as far away as the Pacific Coast. Late in the fourteenth century, the Anasazi simply abandoned their settlements. No one really knows why they left or exactly where they went, but they may have been driven away by drought or warfare. They are

This early twentieth-century painting shows a Zuni pottery-maker at work.

probably the ancestors of at least some of the Pueblo peoples.

By the mid-1300s, the Zuni—whose relationship with the Anasazi remains unclear—were living in a half-dozen large villages along the Zuni River. They lived in large, multistory cliffside dwellings made of stone and farmed in the surrounding area. It was here, two centuries later, that the Zuni first made contact with Europeans.

One of the cliff dwellings built by the mysterious Anasazi people

The Spanish, who had already conquered Mexico to the south, had heard legends about a place of great wealth called the Seven Cities of Cibola. When a group of explorers first saw the Zuni pueblo of Hawikuh in 1539, they believed they had found Cibola. Despite fierce resistance, the Spanish conquered the Zuni and the other Pueblo people, and by 1598, the entire area was under Spanish control.

The Zuni Creation Story

The Zuni believe that their earliest ancestors lived in the deepest and darkest of four "underworlds." They were afraid to climb to the surface of the Earth, which was ravaged by terrible earthquakes and floods and populated by huge animals. But spirits—sometimes called the Children of the Sun—gave the Zuni fire to light their way and sent lightning bolts to stop the earthquakes and clear away the floodwaters. They also turned most of the animals to stone, and the smaller, less dangerous ones that escaped are those that live on the Earth today.

These rock paintings, showing human and animal figures, were created by Zuni ancestors centuries ago.

Spanish explorers enter the Zuni pueblo of Hawikuh in the sixteenth century.

The Pueblo suffered terribly under Spanish rule. Their lands were taken away, their people were forced into slave labor, and many of their leaders were killed. Perhaps most painful for the Pueblo, the Spanish tried to force them to give up their traditional religious practices and become Christians. Finally, in 1680, the Pueblo—including the Zuni—revolted.

It was only after twelve years of bloody fighting that the Spanish finally established permanent control over the Pueblo lands. During the Pueblo Revolt, the Zuni abandoned all but one of their six villages and gathered together in a single pueblo called Halona. This is the place we know today as Zuni Pueblo.

The Zuni continued to hold on to their traditional way of life. They were more successful than some of the other Pueblo peoples, partly because they lived farther away from the main Spanish settlements. In 1848, at the end of the Mexican-American War, the United States took control of a huge expanse of the Southwest that had belonged to Mexico. The U.S. government formally recognized the Zuni's right to their traditional lands around Zuni Pueblo, marking a new chapter in Zuni history.

2 · LIFE IN THE HIGH DESERT

The Zuni are among the world's most skillful farmers. They use highly advanced **irrigation** techniques to grow food on their dry desert lands. They channel water from the Zuni River—and scarce rainfall and **runoff** from the melting snow in the distant mountains—to their fields which are often walled off to preserve the precious water.

The Zuni have always raised corn, beans, and squash—three crops so important that they are known as the three sisters. Corn is especially important. Many different varieties are grown and cooked in many different ways, including soups and stews. One of the most delicious is a paper-thin flatbread called *hewe*. A recipe for *hewe* is one of the most closely guarded secrets of any Zuni cook.

The Zuni did not rely entirely on farming. They also gathered wild plants, such as berries and **yucca**, to use for food,

The Zuni's famous "waffle gardens" make the most of the scarce water in the southwestern desert.

A Zuni family planting crops

medicine, and dyes. And they were excellent hunters. They used bows and arrows, spears, traps, and even slingshots to kill animals as large as bison, deer, elk, and antelope, and as small as prairie dogs and pheasants.

Despite being deeply devoted to their traditional way of life, the Zuni have always been willing to learn from outsiders. The Spanish brought with them horses, donkeys, and oxen, which the Zuni used to work their fields and carry their crops—including new ones, such as wheat, peaches, and chili peppers—to market. They also learned to raise sheep from the

Spanish. Something else that the Spanish introduced is the "beehive" oven, which the Zuni use for cooking to this day.

The hard work of farming, food gathering, and hunting meant that the Zuni were an unusually close-knit people. The Zuni traditionally lived together in large buildings made of stone covered with clay that were sometimes four or five stories high. When the Spanish arrived, the largest Zuni pueblo, Hawikuh, had more than a hundred of these buildings. Their height made it easy for the Zuni to defend themselves against attackers. The lower levels, which were used for storage, usually had no doors or windows. People entered the buildings using ladders that led to the upper levels, which were used as living space. The roofs—made of wood covered with mud— were work areas.

These buildings were occupied by Zuni **clans**—large "extended families" named for animals, plants, or natural forces, such as Eagle, Corn, or Sun. A Zuni clan included grandparents, uncles and aunts, and many other, more distant relations. The clan was matrilineal, which meant that the

Zuni Corn Soup

This simple soup—adapted from a traditional recipe—brings together ingredients that have been important to the Zuni for hundreds, even thousands, of years. Corn has always been one of the most important foods for this farming people: lamb and chili peppers were introduced by the Spanish: and salt is important in both cooking and religion for the Zuni. The result is absolutely delicious. The recipe is easy to make, but you will need an adult to help you cut up the lamb and use the stove.

Ingredients

- 2 cups (500 milliliters) lamb
- 6 cups (1.5 liters) water, divided
- 1½ cups (375 ml) sweet corn, canned or frozen
- 2 teaspoons (10 ml) crushed red chili pepper flakes (if desired)
- 1 teaspoon (5 ml) salt

Cut the lamb into half-inch cubes. Bring three cups (750 ml) of water to a boil in a large pot. Place the lamb in the pot and reduce the heat and simmer until the lamb is tender. Add the corn to the pot, along with the salt and three more cups (750 ml) of water. Add the chili peppers (if you like) and simmer until the corn is just tender and the soup is heated through.

A Zuni pueblo in 1873

mother, not the father, was the head of the household. The clan's house and other property belonged to the mother, not the father, and when a young man married, he went to live with his bride's clan. The clan is still an important element of Zuni culture today.

From the earliest times, the Zuni have been highly skilled artists and craftspeople. Zuni pottery—traditionally decorated with geometric designs and pictures of animals, often in combinations of black, brown, and white—is prized by collectors all over the world. The Zuni also make jewelry from **turquoise**. Today they use silver in place of the tin that they used in the past. They also do needlepoint and inlay work, using stones, shells, and beads to create elaborate jewelry designs.

Among the most famous Zuni art forms are **Kachina** dolls, which represent the spirits worshiped by the Zuni. These small figures are carved from stone, bone, and other materials. They have religious significance for the Zuni, and for other Pueblo peoples, but only if they are blessed by a Zuni priest. They are often given to Zuni children to teach them about the spirits. Small Kachina dolls, often strung on necklaces, are highly prized as souvenirs by visitors to Zuni Pueblo, but these are purely decorative and are not considered religious objects.

This historic photograph shows a Zuni artist decorating a Kachina doll.

The Zuni have always been a deeply religious people. Some experts believe that more than 90 percent of the Zuni people still practice their traditional religion. Many Zuni actually practice these beliefs alongside the religion brought by the Spanish, observing both Zuni rituals and Catholic feast days.

The Zuni worship many gods, but the most important are probably Awonawilona (the creator of all things), Ápoyan Tä'chu (Father Sky), and Awitelin Tsita (Mother Earth). The Zuni also believe that spirits, called Kachinas, are present in everything—in animals and plants, in natural forces such as wind and rain, and in man-made objects such as pottery and baskets. There are many different Kachinas, both good and evil. One is a horrible, hairy creature called the Atoshle. When Zuni children misbehave, their parents

The ruins of a settlement that was abandoned by the Zuni more than seven hundred years ago

A Zuni Kachina doll

sometimes tell them that the Atoshle will come and carry them away in a basket.

The Zuni honor the gods and spirits in religious festivals throughout the year, and also in their daily lives, by praying, singing, dancing, and drumming. Many Zuni religious practices remain mysterious to outsiders, because the Zuni are very secretive about them. For example, even though the Zuni welcome visitors to the Zuni Pueblo, they do not permit them to photograph—or sometimes even watch—religious ceremonies.

For the Zuni, as for many farming peoples—especially

Native Americans take part in a religious ceremony in a kiva.

those living in environments as difficult as the arid deserts of the Southwest—religion is concerned with the welfare of the community as a whole. One of the most important elements is the need to predict and control the weather, and especially to pray for rain, without which crops cannot grow.

Most Zuni belong to one of the pueblo's many religious societies. The most important of these societies are the six kivas. Most Zuni boys become members of one of the kivas or another religious society between the age of eight and twelve. There are other groups, too, including the famous "mud-heads," who perform at the most important event in the Zuni's year—the Shalako Festival.

There are many other special religious events in the Zuni calendar. These include the annual barefoot walk to Zuni Salt Lake, the home of Ma'loyattsik'i or Salt Woman. For as long as anyone can remember, the Zuni and other Pueblo peoples have walked the sacred trails to gather salt for use in their religious ceremonies.

Another place that is sacred to the Zuni is Kolhu/wala:wa,

The Shalako Festival

The Shalako Festival takes place in late November or early December. It marks the end of the Zuni year and the beginning of a new one. The festival begins with clownlike figures called mudheads announcing that the Shalakos—messengers of the Kachinas—are on their way. The Shalakos are represented by people wearing ten-foot-tall costumes that make them look like huge birds. They enter the pueblo to give prayers of thanks for the past year's harvest. Then they dance all night to pray for a good year to come. When the festival ends, the Shalakos leave the pueblo, and the Zuni **fast** for ten days.

a lake in eastern Arizona located about 60 miles (97 kilometers) southwest of Zuni Pueblo. The Zuni believe that a village beneath this lake is where the souls of the Zuni go when they die—and that it is also where the mudheads come from. Every four years, or any time water is very scarce, a group of Zuni walks barefoot to the lake to pray for the well-being of the entire world, not just the Zuni. Their right to cross the lands on this "pilgrimage," which has sometimes been challenged by landowners, is now guaranteed by law.

Make a Zuni Necklace

The Zuni make stone carvings of the animals—such as bears, coyotes, and rabbits—that they worship as spirits, and string them on necklaces. Why not try making your own necklace, using materials you can find in your kitchen or at craft stores? You will need an adult to help you with the oven and the hot bowl.

You will need:

* oven
* 1 sheet of aluminum foil, 1–2 feet (30–60 centimers) long
* table knife or other blunt knife
* 1 or more blocks of modeling compound (Sculpey or other brand, available at craft stores) that hardens when dried in the oven
* toothpicks
* skewer (metal or wood)
* ovenproof bowl (slightly smaller than the skewer)
* potholders
* approximately 1 yard (1 meter) of beading cord (available at craft stores) or dental floss
* 10–20 beads (more can be used if the beads are very small)

(continued on next page)

1· Preheat the oven to the temperature given in the instructions on the package of modeling compound.

2· Lay the sheet of foil on the kitchen counter or table. Use the knife to cut a square of the modeling compound approximately a quarter of an inch (6 millimeters) thick. Then carve the shape of an animal into the square.

3· Stick a toothpick through the middle of the animal, at the thickest point. (If you make a bear, for example, stick it in the stomach and out through the back.) Move the toothpick around a little to make the whole larger. Remove the toothpick.

4· Make more animals, then place them on the skewer, as shown, making sure they do not touch each other. Lay the skewer across the top of the ovenproof bowl.

5. Place the bowl in the oven for the time given in the instructions on the package of modeling compound.

6. Using the potholders, remove the bowl from the oven and set it on the stove (or some other heatproof surface) to cool.

7. Take the beading cord or dental floss and tie a large knot in one end. When the animals are cool, string them, separated by a few beads as shown, on the beading cord or dental floss. Tie another large knot in the other end.

8. Tie the two ends of the beading cord or dental floss together to complete your necklace.

Animal shapes for tracing

4 · A CHANGING WORLD

When the Southwest became part of the United States, the Zuni signed treaties with the federal government. In part they did this because they hoped to gain protection against attacks by their more warlike neighbors, the Apache and especially the Navajo. Despite their bitter experiences with the Spanish, the Zuni were more welcoming to the newcomers crossing their territory than many other native peoples were.

The Zuni supplied food to the U.S. Army soldiers fighting in what came to be known as the **Navajo Wars**. The Zuni sometimes joined in the fighting themselves. They rescued soldiers and settlers who had been attacked by Navajo and Mohave warriors. They also helped the famous Western scout Christopher "Kit" Carson in his exploration of the area. They even gave shelter to some Navajo who had sided with them

A pueblo village in New Mexico, with an old Spanish mission church

Christopher "Kit" Carson was one of the most famous frontiersmen and guides in the old West.

against their own people. There is still a small Navajo enclave, the Ramah Reservation, within the boundaries of the Zuni lands.

By the mid-1860s, the Zuni were mostly safe from attack by their neighbors, and in 1877, the first section of land was formally set aside by the U.S. government for the Zuni Reservation. Two years later the government sent an expedition to study the Zuni's culture and traditions. One member of the expedition, **anthropologist** Frank H. Cushing, lived at Zuni Pueblo for almost five years. He was adopted by the Zuni and was even allowed to join some of their secret religious societies. The books he wrote about them made the Zuni famous across the United States and around the world.

This nineteenth-century engraving shows Frank H. Cushing in traditional Zuni dress.

The Zuni's traditional ways were changing, however. They began to abandon their traditional multistoried homes and move into small single-family houses. They were also changing some of their traditional ways of making a living. In many cases, they gave up the peach orchards that have supported them well since the days of Spanish rule. By the middle of the twentieth century, jewelry and other crafts—sold mainly to outsiders—accounted for more than half of the income earned on Zuni Pueblo.

One of the most important changes for the Zuni came in the 1930s, when they moved away from their traditional form of government. The Zuni had always been ruled by their religious leaders, but in 1934, they introduced democratic government, with an elected tribal council.

The Zuni have always been protected from some of the damage done by outsiders, in part by their geographical isolation. However, the Zuni have suffered—and continue to suffer—from problems that plague other Native American peoples, including poverty, alcoholism, and drug abuse.

The Zuni Language

Many Native American peoples have found it very difficult to preserve their languages, and many Native American languages have few, if any, remaining fluent speakers. But this is not true of the Zuni language, which is completely unrelated to any other language, including the languages of the other Pueblo peoples. The Zuni language's uniqueness is probably one of the reasons it has survived. Zuni is still widely spoken in Zuni homes and throughout Zuni Pueblo, and is taught in the pueblo's schools. Fewer than ten thousand people worldwide speak Zuni. Here are a few common Zuni words:

English	Zuni
Zuni (people)	*A'Shiwi*
Zuni (language)	*Shiwi'ma*
man	*lashik'i*
woman	*mak'i*
sun	*ya'dok'ya*
moon	*yachunne*
water	*ky'awe*

Among the problems the Zuni have had to face since the creation of the Zuni Reservation are repeated attempts by non–Native Americans to take over their lands.

Outsiders—including ranchers and miners—often threatened to take over Zuni lands, but the Zuni have always fought back. In 1935 the federal government agreed to increase the Zuni lands. Today the Zuni Indian Reservation is 723 square miles (1,873 square kilometers). Most of it is located at Zuni Pueblo, but it also includes some other lands that are not attached to the main reservation, in Catron County, New Mexico, and Apache County, Arizona. Most of the approximately 12,000 Zuni still live on or very near the pueblo. During the warm-weather months, some move to three smaller farming villages nearby—Pescado, Nutria, and Ojo Caliente.

Zuni Pueblo is a popular tourist attraction. Visitors from all over the world come to experience Zuni traditions, history, and culture, as well as the natural beauty of the pueblo. The pueblo's attractions include the Old Zuni Mission, a Catholic church from the era of Spanish rule, with famous

A Zuni leader testifies at a congressional hearing in Washington, D.C., about Native American land rights.

wall paintings showing traditional Zuni life; Halona Idiwan'a (the "Middle Village" or "Old Pueblo"); and the Hawikuh Ruins, a U.S. National Historic Landmark. There are also many art galleries and stores where visitors can buy Kachina dolls, jewelry, pottery, baskets, paintings, and other crafts.

Zuni Pueblo is about far more than tourism, however, and for this reason, the Zuni's fight to protect their lands has never

The Old Zuni Mission Church, in the heart of Zuni Pueblo

ended. Recently, the Zuni Salt Lake, one of the most sacred sites to the Zuni and many of the other Pueblo peoples, was threatened by a utility company's plans to build a huge coal mine that would have drained away some of the lake. The Zuni sued, and in 2003 they won their case and plans for the mine were abandoned.

Today, life for the Zuni is changing rapidly. More and more young Zuni now leave the pueblo to attend college, to serve in the military, or to lead lives in the modern, "Western" style. Yet most Zuni still live on or close to the pueblo. Even those who live far away usu-

Zuni perform the traditional deer dance at the Gallup Intertribal Indian Ceremonial.

ally return to attend weddings, funerals, and festivals, and to revisit the old ways. Among the most important events are the Zuni Tribal Fair and the Gallup Intertribal Indian Ceremonial, both held every August. By attending these events, the Zuni face the future without ever abandoning the rich traditions of their great and proud past.

· TIME LINE

Ancient peoples cross a land bridge connecting Asia and the Americas.

The Anasazi (Ancient Pueblo) establish a complex, sophisticated culture, then mysteriously abandon their settlements.

The Zuni people have established settlements along the Zuni River.

Spanish explorers and soldiers from Mexico come into the area and fight the Zuni.

The Spanish complete their conquest of the Zuni and the other Pueblo peoples.

Native Americans rise up against the Spanish in the Pueblo Revolt.

Most of the Zuni abandon their other settlements to live at Halona, which is now known as the Zuni Pueblo.

The Southwest, including the Zuni lands, becomes part of the United States.

| c. 20,000-100,000 | c. 100–1350 | Mid-1300s | 1539–1540 | 1598 | 1680–1692 | 1693–1700 | 1848 |

The U.S. government signs two treaties with the Zuni.

The Zuni are caught up in the Navajo Wars between their neighbors and the U.S. Army.

The first land is set aside for the Zuni Indian Reservation.

The Zuni adopt a democratic form of government, and the federal government expands the Zuni Indian Reservation.

Zuni Salt Lake is returned to Zuni control.

Zuni land claims are settled against the U.S. government, which paid the Zuni $25 million.

The Zuni finally win the battle to save Zuni Salt Lake.

1850–1851   1859–1864   1877   1934–1935   1978   1990   2003

· GLOSSARY

adobe: a building material made of clay and straw and dried in the sun.

Anasazi: an early Native American people of the Southwest (sometimes known as the Ancient Pueblo), who may have been ancestors of the Zuni and some other Pueblo peoples.

anthropologist: a person who studies the physical, social, and cultural characteristics of human beings.

clan: a large "extended family" of people who are related to one another, sometimes distantly (for example, including grandparents, uncles and aunts, and cousins).

crops: plants, such as corn or beans, that are raised for food.

fast: to go without food for an extended period of time.

irrigation: moving and conserving water—for example, with ditches, canals, and walled gardens—for use in farming.

Kachina: one of the spirits worshiped by the Zuni.

kiva: a Zuni religious society, or a pit house–like structure used for Zuni religious practices.

migratory: moving from place to place, usually in search of food.

Navajo Wars: a series of armed conflicts during the 1850s and 1860s between the Navajo people and the U.S. government.

Paleo-Indian: the earliest Native Americans.

pit house: an early type of Pueblo dwelling, made by digging a pit and then covering it with adobe and wood.

Pueblo: a group of culturally related Native American peoples of the Southwest.

pueblo: a village where some Native Americans of the Southwest live.

runoff: water from melting snow.

sedentary: following a settled way of life in a permanent dwelling place.

turquoise: a semiprecious stone used for jewelry making by the Zuni.

yucca: one of a group of plants with edible fruits and flowers that are also sometimes used as medicine.

• FIND OUT MORE

Books

Bjorklund, Ruth. *The Hopi (First Americans)*. New York: Marshall Cavendish Benchmark Books, 2008.

Broida, Marion. *Projects about the Southwest Indians*. New York: Marshall Cavendish Benchmark Books, 2006.

Press, Petra. *The Zuni (First Reports Native Americans)*. Minneapolis: Compass Point Books, 2002.

Websites

Chaco Culture National Historical Park
http://www.nps.gov/chcu

Chronological History of the Zuni
http://www.ashiwi.org/ChronologicalHistory.aspx

Pueblo of Zuni Official Site of the Zuni Tribe
http://www.ashiwi.org

Zuni Minnesota State University EMuseum
http://www.mnsu.edu/emuseum/cultural/northamerica/zuni.html

About the Author

Terry Allan Hicks has written more than a dozen books for Marshall Cavendish Benchmark, including several about Native American peoples. He lives in Connecticut with his wife, Nancy, and their three sons, James, Jack, and Andrew.

• INDEX

Page numbers in **boldface** are illustrations.